MW01119051

THE ENEMY DEPRESSION

FINDING HOPE AND HEALING THROUGH FAITH

DR. SHARON E. HARRIS

The Enemy Depression - Finding Hope and Healing Through Faith

Copyright © 2024 by Dr. Sharon E. Harris

All rights reserved.

No part of this book may be reproduced in any form or by any electronic or mechanical means, including information storage and retrieval systems, without written permission from the author, except for the use of brief quotations in a book review.

Paperback ISBN 979-8-218-37536-2

Book Designed by Brand It Beautifully™ at www.branditbeautifully.com

In loving memory of my mother, Alberta Jackson Rankin, whose unwavering faith sustained her, even in the face of life's adversities. It was her strength and unshakable belief in God's promises that guided me and all of my siblings through.

CONTENTS

INTRODUCTION

"A thief comes but to kill, steal and destroy, but I came that they might have life and have it more abundantly." John 10:10

We have a real enemy who wants to steal your joy. He wants to take your peace and destroy your mind. That enemy is depression. Growing up as a child, I never knew I had depression—it was never diagnosed. As I looked back over my life while wanting to write about depression, its causes, and its effects, I found that it was possible that this disorder had silently entered my life. The things that I went through, the challenges and all the stresses of life, had an effect on me.

I don't know your story. I don't know your hurts or pains, but I believe that I have been through just about every disappointment that this life could offer. A father that walked out when I was a little girl, a husband that called it quits after 10 years, the death of a child, and the death of my mother many years later. There's so much that I cannot write it all. For now, I will share as much as I can recall of the losses, the disappointments, and the setbacks.

This enemy creeps in and says to you, "Where is this life that God has promised you, where you will have things in abundance? Maybe in the afterlife." I couldn't believe that lie. I want to encourage you to trust the God, who kept my mind through it all. Don't allow the enemy to win: Don't let depression steal, kill, or destroy your life.

I know that God will keep you. He will help you and restore the life He has promised. He did it for me, and I know He can do it for you. Just trust in Him and trust His word. You will experience that more abundant life.

CHAPTER ONE

IDENTIFYING THE ENEMY

What is depression? Dr. Pauline Reeder states that it is an illness that takes a great deal of time and energy out of a person's life. It could be caused by genetics, life events, medications, or a medical condition. We, as a society, have seen more cases of depression since the onset of the COVID-19 pandemic. Many have been impacted, but they are afraid to seek help. They remain captive, constantly being taunted. Depression is not prejudiced; it can attack men, women, teens, and children. No specific race or religious group — whether Christians, believers, or non-believers — is exempt.

I believe that not one person today can say they haven't felt some form of depression in their life, whether mild or severe. It is believed by psychologists that, with therapy, counseling, and/or medications such as antidepressants, one can be helped. I also believe that the word of God will help sustain and keep a person focused while undergoing treatment.

WHAT ARE THE SIGNS OF DEPRESSION?

What happens in the brain when someone is depressed? According to Sam's Center for Peak Performance, depression involves the brain's delicate chemistry. More specifically, depression involves chemicals known as neurotransmitters which aid in the transmission of messages between the nerve cells in the brain. Certain neurotransmitters regulate the mood, and if they run low, people can become depressed, anxious, and stressed. Stress can affect the balance in the neurotransmitters and lead to depression.

Adults, teens, children: How does one recognize the symptoms or signs of a depressive disorder? How do we know if someone is going through a state of depression? Here are some common signs to look for according to the National Institute of Mental Health (NIMH):

- Persistent sadness, anxious, and/or empty mood
- Feelings of hopelessness and/or pessimism
- Feelings of guilt, worthlessness, and/or helplessness
- Loss of interest or pleasure in hobbies and activities that were once enjoyed
- Decreased energy, fatigue, and/or being slowed down
- Difficulty concentrating, remembering, and/or making decisions
- Insomnia, early morning waking, and/or oversleeping

- Appetite and weight loss and/or overeating and weight gain
- Thoughts of death or suicide and/or suicide attempts
- Restlessness and/or irritability
- Persistent physical symptoms that do not respond to treatment, such as headaches
- Digestive disorders and/or chronic pain

ADULTS

Many may deny the fact that they are depressed. They often try to hide symptoms to avoid being thought of as mentally ill, and they may complain about physical illnesses such as headaches, stomach pains, and fatigue. Many may become prone to accidents, sometimes hurting themselves rather than others. According to Dr. Reeder, in some cases they may engage in excessive drinking, gambling, and sexual promiscuity.

TEENS AND CHILDREN

Depression is a significant mood disorder that has the potential to rob a child of the joy in their life. Experts used to think that only adults could suffer from depression. However, now we know that even a young child can develop a depression disorder that requires treatment. As many as three in 100 children and nine in 100 teens have serious depression. Still, many do not get the treatment they need. It can be hard to tell the difference between depression and normal moodiness, and it may not look the same in teens as it does in an adult. An older child may be sad, grumpy, or bored most of the time, and they may not take pleasure in things they used to enjoy. A depressed young person may lose or gain weight, sleep too much or too little, and feel hopeless, worthless, or guilty. Some turn to drugs and alcohol. They may think about death or suicide a lot.

Very young children may lack energy and become withdrawn; any feelings of hopelessness or trouble sleeping should be looked into right away. Grade-school children may have many headaches or upset stomachs, and they may lose interest in their friends and activities. With young children and teens, parents should pay close attention in case they have been abused or molested. Many times, depression arises because they cannot talk about what has happened to them. They often try to avoid going to school or hanging out with close friends.

TYPES OF DEPRESSION

There are a few different types of depression. I will list a few common types of depressive disorders. Bipolar disorder, also known as manic depressive disorder, is characterized by cycling mood changes, from severe high (manic periods) to severe lows (depressive periods). When in a mania cycle, the individual may be overactive, overly talkative, and have a great deal of energy. Mania often affects one's thinking. Those impacted by bipolar disorder often exhibit social behaviors that can cause serious problems in both public and private settings, many times causing embarrassment.

Major depressive disorder (clinical depression) or unipolar depression is manifested by a combination of systems that interfere with the ability to work, study, sleep, eat, and enjoy once-pleasurable activities. This disabling episode of depression may occur only once, but it more commonly occurs several times in a person's lifetime. A less severe type of depression is called dysthymia, which involves long-term, chronic systems that do not disable a person but keep them from functioning well or feeling good.

According to [NIMH] Other types of depressive disorders are erogenous, psychotic, chronic, or reactive.

- Reactive depression comes as a reaction to a traumatic event in a person's life. This event may be real or imaginary.
- Erogenous depression is believed to arise due to a person's ability (or lack thereof) to attain certain goals.
- Psychotic depression is a type of disorder that may grant elevated levels of anxiety. Individuals with this form of depression are not usually destructive.
- Chronic depression is of a lengthy duration. The acute form may last for shorter periods of time with differing levels of intensity.

CAUSES OF DEPRESSION

GENETICS

Research shows that depression runs in families, and some people inherit genes that make it more likely for them to get depressed. Not everyone who has the genetic make up for depression gets depressed. However, many people who have no family history of depression still have the condition. Therefore, although genes are one factor, they are not the single cause.

LIFE EVENTS

The death of a loved one, friend, or even a pet can cause a person to go beyond normal grief and lead to depression. It could be a divorce or separation, while the re-marrying of a parent can also trigger depression in children and teens.

MEDICAL CONDITIONS

Certain medical conditions can affect hormone balance and therefore mood. Some conditions, such as hypothyroidism, are also known to cause a depressed moods in some people. When these medical conditions are diagnosed and treated by a doctor, the depression usually disappears.

CHANGES IN SITUATIONS

As stated before, life events can be a cause of depression such as a person losing their job and no longer being able to care for their family. Or a new move to another state or town, with no family or friends nearby, could also cause loneliness. There could be a sudden illness which could cause one to incur major debt from hospital bills. Likewise, the news of a terminal illness and only six months to live may trigger depression. Pauline Reeder, author of "*God's Power to Help Hurting People*," lists many other events. It could be the arrival of a new baby, wherein the other siblings could become depressed or feel neglected and even jealous. Many young people run away from home so as to not face problems with parents or stepparents.

DEATH OF A LOVED ONE/KIDNAPPING OF A CHILD

The parents will become depressed through not knowing where their child may be. Seeing other children can deepen the depression. Rape, molestation, child abuse, and domestic violence can also all cause a reaction of depression, whether male or female. Depression can lead a person to live an abnormal life. In any of these situations, help should be sought immediately. Abuse and domestic violence are serious problems today, and most people do not want to talk about it. Some even try to hide it. Reeder said, "They hide in fear and depression." Domestic violence is a very serious matter that can lead to accidental death and murder. Anyone experiencing these types of situations should seek help immediately.

LONELINESS

Reeder mentioned people who are left alone without human contact for long periods of time. Homelessness and extreme fatigue are two other situations that can cause depression. Extreme fatigue is caused by overwork, long hours, and no vacations or breaks. Many people push themselves to the point that they break down. Thankfully, this can be cured by long vacations or breaks, doing things that a person enjoys in life, and taking time to relax for a while. *[Pauline Reeder, God's Power to Help Hurting People; NIMH]*

The good news is - all hope is not lost! Depression is a treatable disorder, and I encourage treatment in the form of education, counseling, or therapy. It should never be ruled out. A person with depression must realize that getting treatment is very important, as depression not only affects the person but their family as well. Help is always available for all who seek it. It is said that some try to harm themselves or others in the belief that how they feel will never change. This is why I call it **the enemy**; it wants to leave one believing the lie of hopelessness and helplessness.

Now that we know some of the types of depression, I would advise seeking a diagnosis from a physician.

Equip yourself with the proper treatment and the word of God to fight the enemy. No one should feel alone; there is help.

CHAPTER TWO

DEPRESSION IN THE BIBLE

After having looked at the various types and symptoms of depression, I speculate that people in the Bible may have suffered from this disorder. These individuals include Mary, Martha, the prophet Elijah, Hannah, and even King David, to name a few.

MARY AND MARTHA

These women experienced the death of a loved one. When death hits a family, one cannot truly explain how they feel. Emotions are unsettled, with ups and downs, emptiness, and pain. Each person goes through this experience differently. I believe Mary had feelings of hopelessness, sadness, and even some guilt. Perhaps she felt she hadn't gotten the message to their friend Jesus early enough. Maybe she thought her brother would have had more time and would have gotten better, but he only grew worse.

Their friend Jesus would surely come right away. However, when Lazarus died, Martha and Mary went into depression. The Bible does not say that they were depressed, but let's look at the symptoms.

Death triggers feelings of hopelessness and unbearable anguish. Their brother had just died. He had been sick for a very long time, and the family friend, whom they loved, had not come.

John 11:20 states, "Now Mary stayed in the house, Martha complained to Jesus, if you had been here my brother would not have died."

Martha showed signs of sadness, anger, and hopelessness. Mary, on the other hand, stayed in the house and withdrew. I see two people in a depressive state, displaying two different reactions. Martha is angry and wants someone to blame, even showing signs of irritability. Mary is withdrawn and does not want to leave the house. She shows a lack of interest when their longtime friend arrives, as if to say, "What's the use? You are too late!"

In the passing of my nephew, my sister had the same reaction as Mary. She withdrew, and she wanted to neither see anyone nor leave her house.

When we look to Jesus, one will find He is a comforter and great counselor. He spoke calmly and was patient with Mary and Martha. It was through Christ's patience —His words of comfort, hope, truth, and reassurance— that Mary and Martha gained their faith.

Christ did, in fact, raise Lazarus from the dead, because He Himself is the resurrection. It was for the people's benefit that this miracle was performed. Jesus proved that He was who He said He was—and still is.

We can help the grieving individual by showing compassion, just as Jesus did with Mary and Martha. Lend a listening ear and share a word of comfort.

Psalm 30:11-12 "One day he will turn our mourning into gladness."

Revelation 21:4 "He will wipe away every tear from their eyes and death shall be no more."

Life's challenges will take time, even though one may feel as if they are all alone. Having a good friend in these times of sorrow will be of great comfort. The enemy was defeated for Mary and Martha.

ELIJAH THE PROPHET

This man of God could have suffered from depression also, based on our readings of the scripture. Elijah showed signs of despair, hopelessness, loss of appetite, oversleeping. and thoughts of death. [1 Kings 19:1-14]

Elijah was threatened by a queen named Jezebel. He killed four hundred of the false prophets, and Queen Jezebel told him that the same fate awaited him. This man ran for his life. When he found himself about a day's journey into the wilderness, Elijah sat down under a tree, exhausted and afraid. He prayed that he might die.

Depression can cause one to wish death (suicide) on themselves, as they may feel or believe that there is no way out of a situation. There seems to be no other alternative. This is how the enemy blinds people: By attacking the mind, the victim feels there is only one way out.

Elijah falls asleep, with the enemy of depression trying to overtake him. He won't eat, he won't drink, and he has no appetite.

We may know of someone who is showing these signs. They may be going through a difficult time in their life and have feelings of despair. For Elijah, an angel of the Lord wakes him, gives him drink, and tells him to eat. Soon after eating, he sleeps again.

As God had a plan for Elijah life, so too does He have a plan for others.

The angel wakes him again and tells him to eat, because he has a long journey ahead of him. Elijah wants to give up, but the angels shake him again and tell him to eat and get up. God has a plan for his life.

If one gets the help that is available and applies the word of God, they will find that their life is of value. The word of God speaks, if we listen. He tells us who we are and that we are valuable.

Jeremiah 29:11 ""For I know the plans I have for you," declares the LORD, "plans to prosper you and not harm you, plans to give you a hope and a future.""

That's good news for someone who is fighting this disorder: There is always hope in God's word! I truly believe it will help someone get though times of difficulties. Elijah found that God had many more prophets in addition to himself, whom he had hidden in a cave. Elijah was not alone. If God is for you, no one can be against you! Stay encouraged when you face difficulties. Jesus said, "I will never leave you nor forsake you." One must believe they are not alone.

I Peter 5:7 states, "Cast your cares on him for he cares for you."

The prophet had God with him, and God delivered him from danger.

In the Bible, there were no doctors as we have today—no group therapy or counselors. We have all that we need and the word of God to keep us from the enemy of depression. There is help, be it physical, mental, or spiritual. My advice is to trust in God, who can deliver you and keep you from the enemy's hands.

A SAMARITAN WOMAN

The Bible never speaks her name, but she is a woman of shame. She has been looked down upon by many because of prejudices relating to her race and her lifestyle. She was of a mixed blood, being half Hebrew and Assyrian. Her lifestyle was of many relationships and possibly five marriages. When a person is looked down upon because of race, it can cause them to suffer some form of depression. They may show signs of despair, restlessness, or anxiety. This woman had an emptiness that no one could fulfill. Because of her many relationships, she may have suffered from low self-esteem.

In the Bible, this woman came to a well to draw water. Most women came early in the morning, but she came late in the afternoon to avoid the whispers. As she looked up, the man Jesus was there. He asked her for a drink of water. As a conversation took place between them, she asked, "Why are you speaking to me?" She had been looked down upon and talked about so often because of her race. It was strange that this man would even speak to her. She did not know what to expect.

So, why did Jesus stop and speak to her? He told her to go and get her husband. The woman replied, "I have no husband." (John 4:6). This scripture in the Bible speaks of the man Jesus seeing all the hurt and pain this woman had been going through. It tells of the love of God that can fill the deepest hurts and pains in one's life. He is the kind of friend who does not judge past mistakes; He offers forgiveness, peace, and love. He spoke to her very soul and gave her all that she needed. This woman's life was changed when she met Jesus.

The enemy had her bound and confused in her mind. She believed that having relationship after relationship would make her happy. She believed the lies of the enemy: that no one cared about her, that she was worthless. You may know a person who is suffering from depression and has low self-esteem. They may be manic depressive and not understand why they do the things that they do. The right treatment, medication, and the word of God will give them the joy and peace that they may have been seeking. Jesus gave her the opportunity to talk about her problems with Him. He is a great counselor, and He let her know who she was in Him.

Psalm 139:14 "We are fearfully and wonderfully made, marvelous in His eyes."

The word of God can bring joy back to the soul.

HANNAH: A WOMAN CHILDLESS

In I Samuel 1:18, Hannah was barren, meaning she had no children. She was a woman who loved God and worshiped Him.

Depression? The Bible said she worshiped and loved God, so how could she be depressed? Many Christians can become depressed; the enemy does not discriminate. Most feel, "If I pray hard or read the word, this feeling will go away." I have felt this way at one point of my life. One must remember that depression is an illness. We go to the doctor when we get sick: He prescribes medication, we take it, and we get well. If it doesn't work, the doctor prescribes a different medication. So it is with depression: We need the right treatment and the right medication.

Faith plays a big part. God has given wisdom and knowledge to physicians, but as believers, we should seek the proper diagnosis and get the help that we need, then allow God's healing scriptures of His word to manifest in our lives. This is when our faith comes in. Faith is the antibiotic that clears everything up.

Hannah went to the temple, crying unto the Lord. When the priest saw her, he first assumed she was with wine. Hannah told him, "No, sir, my heart was praying unto the Lord!" She was sad, hopeless, and grieved. She had a loss of appetite and suffered restlessness. It was considered a curse if one could not have children. The priest honored her request and took it to the Lord. He told her that by the next year, she would be with child. Hannah went away happy, telling the priest she would give the child back to the Lord if He granted her petition. Although Hannah came to the temple bitter and with anguish, she sought the Lord for help in her situation.

When a believer feels that they are falling into depression, they can begin to pray and ask God for direction. "Help me, guide me to the right source." A knowledgeable pastor or church leader can recommend church counsel or a therapist. They can also offer prayer and encouraging words to comfort the person. Hannah received her blessing from the Lord, just as the priest had said. She was delivered from the enemy of depression because she believed God. She waited and trusted in Him.

Sometimes, when seeking God for children, it may mean praising Him and waiting at the same time. He may allow a natural birth, or it may be through adoption, but either way, one needs to keep the faith. God will deliver or answer in the way He chooses. Don't let the enemy steal the joy or promises of God.

KING DAVID: A MAN AFTER GOD'S OWN HEART

The one who killed the lion and the bear, the one who slew Goliath the giant—David wrote many of the psalms of the Bible, being songs of praise, songs of prayer, and songs of sadness. David had many trials and test. He knew God, but did he battle depression?

Psalm 138 is a psalm of declarative praise attributed to David. He praised God because of an overwhelming answer to the prayer of the king.

> *"I will praise you, oh God, with my whole heart. Before the gods, I will sing praises to you, I will worship towards your holy temple and praise your name, for your loving kindness and your truth, for you have magnified your word above your name. In the day I cried out, you answered me and made me bold with strength in my soul."*

Depression is the enemy.

David in the Bible knew God. When he felt anxious, he knew who to call on. It helps to know who you can call on in times of trouble and despair. Even children of God fall short sometimes. We forget that there is a savior who can help and heal us, and we can call on Him at any time. We often say, "I know God, but I feel so alone. My problems are overwhelming. My burdens are too much for me to bear. I should be stronger than this." Then we ask ourselves, "Am I trusting God? Why do I feel this way, so hopeless and helpless?"

Before David became king, I believe he had to fight a battle of the mind. He was living in the palace with King Saul, but Saul had a jealous spirit directed against David. David fought many battles in the king's army. When Saul became distraught, David would play his harp to soothe his soul. When that evil spirit came over Saul, he tried to pin David to a wall with his spear.

David had thought all was well between he and Saul, and he had formed a friendship with Johnathan, Saul's son. Now he found himself running for his life. Alone and afraid, separated from his family and friends, there's no doubt he was saddened, heartbroken, at a loss, and confused. Having lost friends, having been abused and mistreated, and experiencing sadness... These symptoms can trigger depression.

Just as in David's life, one can experience many challenges. One must face this enemy and not let depression defeat them. I believe and trust in God, so I recognize the signs and receive the help that is necessary. The battle can be won. So many people in the Bible have suffered with many of the same problems we experience today. In the end, they held on to God's promise: "I will never leave you nor forsake you."

PAUL - A MAN CHANGED

There is truly a God who loves and cares deeply for His children, even if it seems that He is far off. In Romans 8:35 (NKJV), Paul the apostle wrote, "Who or what can separate us from the love of Christ? Shall tribulation, or distress, or persecution, or famine, or nakedness, or peril, or sword? As it is written we are killed all day long. We are counted as sheep for the slaughter, yet in all these things we are more than conquers through Him who loved us."

As you read this scripture, Paul continues to say, "Nothing can separate us from the love of God."

This is the reason I believe one can fight off the enemy of depression. Stand on God's word; stand on His promises to get you through all the difficulties of life. This passage of scripture lists all the things that can distract you and steal your focus away from winning the battle. This is a war to take you out, take your mind, and steal your peace. I encourage you to stand bold and declare, "With God on my side, no weapon formed against me shall prosper!" This enemy does not want you to seek the help and treatment that God has provided.

Proverbs 12:25 states, "The anxiety in the heart of man causes depression." This is the only scripture I found in the Bible that mentions depression, but it stands as proof that it is real and people suffer with it. The commentary explanation states, "Anxiety loses some of its force in face of positive encouraging words."

In Acts 9:26-27, Barnabas' encouragement of Paul is a great example of this. "Then when Saul had come to Jerusalem, he tried to join the disciples; but they were all afraid of him, and did not believe that he was a disciple. But Barnabas took him and brought him to the apostles. And he declared to them how he had seen the Lord on the road, and that he had spoken to him, and how he had preached boldly at Damascus in the name of Jesus."

Even Saul, whose name was changed to Paul, had a bout with depression. After being blinded on the road to Damascus, Saul suffered many things. He was a leader who was now being lead. He had to be taken care of by a complete stranger; Saul had to put his trust in someone else besides himself.

After his conversion, Paul was strengthened and filled with the Holy Spirit, so he went and preached the word of Jesus Christ. This was strange, coming from a man who would destroy entire households that confessed Christ. He was basically friendless and lonely. Because of Saul's bad reputation, his murderous acts, and his persecution of the Church, people were afraid of him. He found himself all alone, now that he was on the side of God.

We may find ourselves alone (either because of good decisions or bad ones), but loneliness can cause one to suffer from depression. Being an encouraging friend can help someone overcome depression. Barnabas was that friend to Paul. He told the others how Saul had changed, and he was a witness to that fact.

We need people to help us get through the rough and depressing times in our lives. I pray this book will be powerful and encouraging to you. We need people, physicians, and friends to encourage us along the way when we are hurting or facing difficulties.

CHAPTER THREE

MY STORY

A t a young age, I didn't realize the enemy of depression had already hit our home. My parents decided to separate. There were five of us—four girls and one boy. I can't really recall if my two little sisters were affected by the separation till later on. I do know that my little brother became very angry and rebellious. My mother cried all the time. Signs of depression: sadness, anxious, emptiness, hopelessness, and despair. My dad came to my room one night and said, "I have to leave." This had to be a dream.

We were a perfect family that attended church regularly. Mother stayed home, and Dad went to work every day. Sunday dinners—we would all gather together, bless our meal, and have family talks. Life was good so I thought. Some weekends Dad would take us for a car ride, either into the city or to the air-force field to watch the jets take off. We had trips to the zoo and family vacations. Why was he leaving us?

Depression and anxiety are a hidden force. Studies show that a person who has a depressive disorder is not the only one hurting, as those around them suffer. My mother seemed to slow down. There were no more family dinners and the replacements were those TV dinners in a box. She had lost her energy to cook dinner and cried a lot. It was very difficult for her. I don't believe she was treated for depression until a few years later.

It was a few months later that we found out Dad wasn't coming back.

Depression can steal time away from those who suffer from this disorder. My brother felt the effects of the separation. Children were seldom diagnosed with depression in those days. My brother would stay out late, my mom would worry, and my sister and I would have to go look for him. Most of the time he was throwing rocks down at the creek bed. As time went on, my brother was missing his dad. He became angry at times and would kick the walls or throw things at us. My mother would call my father to come get him, but he only came and talked to him. Then he would leave again.

I believe my brother was depressed. He was very sad and angry most of the time. Mom was sleeping a lot and crying most days, while my older sister and I did what we could to help dress and care for the two little ones . How did we cope? We still had our church family (well, some of them), our pastor, and our neighbor—she helped my mom out a lot. Her boys would play with my brother and keep him out of trouble most of the time.

THE ENEMY COMES TO KILL, STEAL, AND DESTROY

It seemed Mom was getting better. It was holiday time, and Mom was going to cook a turkey for Thanksgiving. She prepared it and placed it in the oven. We put the record player on, then sang and danced. It was happy times again.

Later in the night, my older sister woke me up saying she smelled smoke. We jumped up and found mom asleep on the couch. The record was skipping on this one song, **"What becomes of the broken-hearted / Who had love that's now departed?"** over and over. It was non-stop. To this very day, I can still sing that song! Those memories make me want to cry. Just knowing how my mom suffered was heartbreaking.

My sister was shaking my mom. She sat up and began to cry, "I burnt the turkey," over and over! When I recall these things, I still can feel the pain of my mom. She became more depressed that day, I believe.

Sometimes a situation has to get worse before you realize that you need professional help. I don't know what happened—all I know is that my mother was taken to the hospital by ambulance. She received treatment for depression. She never realized how bad this illness was, nor the effect it was having on her children. My mom learned it was okay to get help, and she decided that we were all going back to church. I can say it was because of the help she received and the word of God that was planted in her heart. Our mom went back to school, received her GED, and began working at one of the top electronics plants in California. I thank God for saving my mother's life and restoring her mind.

As a small child, I think my brother was still experiencing depression. A boy missing his dad. Now that Mom was better, she began to reach out to my father more to spend time with his son. My mom got my brother into Pop Warner football, and Dad would come to the games and watch him play. This was a time for bonding. My brother was only 6 years old when my dad left, and he really needed him in his life. Things were good. My brother was an awesome player—he could run that ball and no one could catch him! However, trouble comes, and the enemy was waiting at the door. It still had a hold on my brother.

When Dad couldn't attend a game, my brother would act up in school and run back to the creek bed, where he would throw rocks. When we got him home, he would kick the walls. Mom couldn't handle this. She called my dad to pick him up, and my dad's response was, "I can't right now."

I don't know if my brother was ever treated for depression, but my mother's faith and prayers must have got him through. At this time, I was to be my brother's best friend. I had to put away my dolls, and I traded them in for GI Joe. We climbed trees, jumped off the playhouse roof, and played Batman and Robin.

My thoughts were, "When can I go back to being a girl?"

Enough was enough. Dad finally came through. He had my brother every other weekend. The joy of the Lord is my strength.

OUR DYSFUNCTIONAL FAMILY: THE HIDDEN ENEMY OF DEPRESSION

A dysfunctional family is characterized by conflict, misbehavior, or abuse. Relationships between members are tense and can be filled with neglect, yelling, and screaming. You might feel forced to happily accept negative treatment.

I may not give an account of all the details of my family life as a child, teen, or young adult, but I believe that the things we went through did have an effect on each of our lives. Our family suffered. There were many days, months, and even years of problems—too many to write about.

Depression can be carried into your adult life if never treated. The decisions that we made as young adults, I believe, were attributed to the childhood depression that we suffered — abandonment issues, anger issues, and low self-esteem. We didn't turn to drugs or alcohol growing up, and we didn't rebel against authority or end up in jail. Still, we had our own demons to fight.

My other siblings have their own stories to tell, but I can reflect on a few.

THE ENEMY COMES, AGAIN, TO KILL, STEAL, AND DESTROY

My eldest sister married into an abusive relationship that ended in divorce. Was this the after-effect of living with childhood depression? She personally had to face depression as an adult when her only child was murdered. That took three years out of my sister's life, and she had to get professional counseling. After her therapy, she was helped through a women's ministry group at our church.

One of my younger siblings attended Harvard University. She was smart, intelligent, and loved God with all her heart, mind, and soul, yet depression was still attached to her subconscious. After college, she allowed the enemy to drag her into an unproductive relationship. It ended in verbal abuse. She didn't realize who she was, as this person had dominated her until she believed she was broken. I didn't think that childhood depression had such an impact on our lives. I don't recall her attending therapy, but she was a prayer warrior and had teachers and friends who were able to encourage her.

Our baby sister was the complete opposite. No one could tell her what do, and she had developed anger issues. I kind of admired her strength. She didn't allow anyone to define her, and her anger protected her from emotional abuse. My little sister was a fighter—and I mean a real fighter. She wouldn't back down from any confrontation, and she would challenge you in a hot second. I believe it was God who saved her. She devoted her life to Christ at 19 years of age.

It seemed my brother, as an adult, had dealt with his problems as a child. Perhaps it was because he was the only one who acted them out while he was younger. He did enlist in the navy at 18, so perhaps the structure of the military changed him.

I married my high-school sweetheart at a young age. For me, I wanted that perfect family that was stolen from me as a child. I recall telling myself, "I will show my parents how to stay married," believing I had all the answers to life at 16. By the time I turned 18, I had a daughter, a husband, and no God. He had abandoned me when He allowed my father to walk out. I was on my own now, and I could live my life the way I wanted. It just took love, hard work, and determination.

I did graduate from high school and college, as I didn't want to suffer the way my mother did. I had it all figured out.

Little did I know, I needed God more than ever. After my college graduation, I found a good job and took care of my family so that my husband could return to school. He had a scholarship to SCC Sacramento. After two weeks of school, he decided that he was too smart for it. He didn't agree with the professors, deans, or counselors, and my wonderful marriage became emotional abuse. I was put down constantly and suffered silently. My family had no idea what was going on in my life.

I had to return to my foundation. I would dress the kids and go to church on Sundays. The praise songs and the worship were exactly what I needed. This gave me peace of mind, even if it was for just one hour. I would leave the church before the word of God was spoken—I didn't want my husband to get upset if I was late coming home.

The kids enjoyed church. It became a part of us. One Sunday, the Pastor said, "Don't anyone leave; I have an important message for today." That is when I had to stay and hear God's word. The word changed my life, as it gave me hope again. I knew God was always with me, even if my father had left.

I say all this because the enemy of depression deals with your mind. I was now experiencing freedom in my heart and mind. The word gave me strength—the strength to face what was ahead of me. My relationship with my husband became more abusive. Once it became physical, I had to leave that relationship for the sake of my children's and my own safety.

CHAPTER FOUR

THE WORD - YOUR WEAPON AGAINST THE ENEMY

A s I have stated before, depression is a mental state of the mind. It is an illness that can be treated. God has given man the wisdom and the knowledge to study and research. God is the author of science, which gives man the ability to make drugs and medications to alter the symptoms of this terrible disease. Man can treat, but God will heal.

MATTHEW 17:14-17

"When they came to the crowd, a man approached Jesus and knelt before him. "Lord, have mercy on my son," he said, "He has seizures and is suffering greatly. He often falls into the fire or into the water. I brought him to your disciples, but they could not heal him." Jesus is speaking, "bring the boy to me!" Jesus rebuked the demon, and it came out of the boy, and he was healed from that moment." **Jesus is a healer.**

MATTHEW 8:28

"When he arrived at the other side in the region of Gadarenes, two demon-possessed men coming from tombs met him. They were so violent that no one could pass that way. "What do you want with us, Son of God!?" They shouted. Have you come here to torture us before the appointed time?" He said "go!" So, they came out and went into pigs, and the whole herd rushed down the steep bank into the lake and died in the water." The people in this town were more concerned about the loss of the pigs than the state of mind of the men who were delivered by Jesus.

The word of God tells us to guard our hearts and our minds. The Christian believer should understand that we have a valid enemy who is out to steal, kill, and destroy our mind, body, and soul. There will be problems and circumstances that we cannot solve, but we know the problem solver.

JAMES 1:2

"Consider it pure joy, my brothers whenever you face trials of many kinds, because you know that the testing of your faith develops perseverance. Perseverance must finish its work so that you may be mature and complete."

JAMES 1:12

"Blessed is the man who perseveres under trials, because when he has stood the test, he will receive the crown of life that God has promised to those who love him."

Our trials are not in vain, the word of God is to keep us focus, and our minds stayed on Jesus.

WORDS FOR GRIEF

When death takes a friend or loved one, we grieve. Embracing Psalm 30:5 can help us to go through the grieving process: "Weeping may endure for the night but joy comes in the morning." God promises repeatedly, "I will never leave you nor forsake you." We can stand on God's promises, for He will never fail us. Nothing about this life did Christ say would be easy, especially for the believer. We would be talked about, scorned, mistreated, mocked, and despised. And why not? Are we any greater than our Master?

The enemy depression will have us believe that there is no hope, but there is hope in God. Christ promised to be with us until the end. He promised us a comforter, which is the Holy Ghost. While we are here, the Spirit of God will help us overcome anything; we must trust Him and keep our faith. Only the word can truly keep us from falling.

David said in Psalm 119, "Your word I have hidden in my heart that I may not sin against you. We need the word hidden in our hearts to fight off depression."

PSALM 51:10-11

"Create in me a clean heart O' God and renew a steadfast spirit within me Do not cast me away from your presence. And do not take your Holy Spirit from me. The Holy Spirit is what keeps us! This is a Psalm, pleading with the Lord to keep us, without him, we would lose our minds."

EPHESIANS 6:10-17

"Finally be strong in the Lord and in his mighty power. Put on the full armor of God so that you can take your stand against the devil's schemes. For our struggles is not against flesh and blood, but, against the rulers, against the authorities, against powers of this dark world and against the spiritual forces of evil in heavenly realms. Therefore, put on the full armor of God, so that when the day of evil [depression] comes you may be able to stand your ground, and after you have done everything to stand, stand firm, then with the belt of truth buckled around your waist, with the breastplate of righteousness in place. And with your feet fitted with the readiness that comes from the gospel of peace in addition to all this, take up the shield of faith, with which you can extinguish all the flaming arrows of the evil one. Take the helmet of salvation and the sword of the Spirit, which is the word of God. The helmet is the word of God, which protects our minds from the lies of the devil. And pray in the spirit on all occasions with all kinds of prayers and request. With this in mind, be alert and always keep praying for all the saints." We must be alert to the devil's tricks and praying always, that we may not be led astray.

God has a purpose and a plan for each one of us. Knowing this can help us to stay focus and in our right minds.

PHILIPPIANS 4:6-7

"Be anxious for nothing but in everything by prayer and supplication, with thanksgiving, let your request be known to God; and the peace of God, which surpassed all understanding, will guard your hearts and minds through Christ Jesus." When we are focused on our Lord and savior Jesus Christ, there is nothing that we can't do.

PHILIPPIANS 4:13

"I can do all things through Christ Jesus who strengthens me."

As children of the most-high God, we can overcome depression and seek help from professionals, Christian counselors, our pastors, and our church body. Don't let the devil fool you into not getting the help and treatment that you may need. Read God's word; it is life, it is comfort, and it gives us peace. We need to know or find out the purpose and plan the Lord has for your life. Every one of God's children should know that we are fearfully and wonderfully made. We were created for God's glory, and we are created to praise, worship, and adore Him. He is to be revered and honored. Through Him, worlds were created. We are created to spread the good news of the gospel.

MATTHEW 28:18

"Then Jesus came to them and said, "All authority in heaven and one earth has been given to me. Therefore; go and make disciples of all nations, baptizing them in the name of the Father and of the Son and of the Holy Ghost and teaching them to obey everything, I have commanded you. And surely, I am with you always, to the very end of the age.""

If we allow the enemy to destroy our minds with the disease of depression, how are we to go and do what the Father has commanded us to do? Satan has no respect for people. He wants God's children to be helpless, hopeless, anxious, restless, irritable, suicidal, and empty. When we are in this state of mind, we are useless, and the work and the will of God cannot go forth. This devil wants us so troubled that we can't do anything to build up God's kingdom.

I JOHN 4:4

"Greater is he that is in me then he that is in the world."

MATTHEW 6:33-34

"But seek first the kingdom of God and his righteousness and all these things shall be added to you. Therefore don't worry about tomorrow, for tomorrow will worry about its own things."

When the enemy of depression gets the saints of God down, we must begin to praise our way through. Don't fall into the trap; recognize the symptoms!

PSALM 146:1-8 (AMPC)

"Praise the Lord! (Hallelujah!) Praise the Lord, O my soul! While I live will I praise the Lord; I will sing praises to my God while I have any being. Put not your trust in princes, in a son of man, in whom there is no help. When his breath leaves him, he returns to his earth; in that very day his [previous] thoughts, plans, *and* purposes perish. Happy (blessed, fortunate, enviable) is he who has the God of [special revelation to] Jacob for his help, whose hope is in the Lord his God, Who made heaven and earth, the sea, and all that is in them, Who keeps truth *and* is faithful forever, Who executes justice for the oppressed, Who gives food to the hungry. The Lord sets free the prisoners, The Lord opens the eyes of the blind, the Lord lifts up those who are bowed down, the Lord loves the [uncompromisingly] righteous (those upright in heart and in right standing with Him)." When we are helpless and in need, our God will take care of us.

PHILIPPIANS 4:8-9 (NKJ)

"Finally, my brethren whatever things are true whatever things are lovely, whatever things are of a good report, if any virtue and anything praiseworthy think on these things! Our God is worthy to be praised in all situations."

Begin to read God's promises. Pray and praise some more. Just as Paul said, we've got to press our way. Press toward the mark of the high calling! God's got a calling on us, which is in Jesus Christ! – Philippians 3:14.

We must remember our destiny. When the enemy of depression comes in like a flood, remember to press your way through it. This is a battle of the mind!

CHAPTER FIVE

RESTORATION CAN BE YOURS

D epression can be a very cruel enemy. He takes everything that he can and leaves one hopeless. He does not play fair. He wants to keep you down, drain you, and take your joy, peace, and happiness. STEAL, KILL, DESTROY! That's his plan. I will not fall; it is time to get help! Don't let the enemy win or kill you!

"Many are the afflictions of the righteous: but the lord delivers him out of them all." Psalm 34:19

During my struggle with the enemy, I did get Christian counseling, and it was what I needed. I attended Bible studies and women's group meetings, and I was learning to love myself and know that I am fearfully and wonderfully made. I cannot express the importance of treatment for depression. There are so many avenues of treatment.

There is help. I cannot express this enough.

This enemy of depression wants to destroy lives and leave one hopeless. That's what it did to me; I was hopeless and helpless.

God has so much more waiting for anyone who will seek Him.

You need only "Ask and it shall be given you. Seek and you will find Knock and the door will be opened for you." Matt. 7:7

I call the Bible the medication for our soul.

DO NOT SUFFER ALONE IN SILENCE

Tell someone if you are feeling despair, stress, or anxiety. Don't try to do it alone. Follow up with a doctor so that they may diagnosis the symptoms. Everyone feels some form of depression from time to time, and it is nothing to be ashamed of. I was ashamed—I couldn't tell my family about my abusive relationship, but the word of God pulled me through. So many lives are destroyed because, as women, we keep silent (that's another story, but it's the truth). Get out of an abusive relationship.

WE WIN IN THE END

My life really turned around. The Lord sent me a man after His own heart. He cares for me and my children. Sometimes you have to wait patiently on God. My husband became a minister of the gospel shortly after we were married, and He truly loves the Lord. We have worked together in the food ministry and prison ministry. We are blessed because we have reached many souls for God's kingdom. God did not forget about me.

The enemy of depression wanted me to give up on life, but God did not leave me out of His plan. He has gifted me with the chance to write plays and teach women, men, boys, and girls of His wonderful love. I established a ministry of praise dance, flag banners, and prayer, and I named it "*ROSE OF SHARON MINISTRIES*," where Christ is the center. If we allow depression to bind us and hold us captive, we will miss out on all the wonderful plans God has for our lives. How will one know if they are not set free from the chains of the enemy?

My siblings are doing awesome works for the Lord. The youngest is married to a minister of the gospel, and they both have doctorates in Biblical studies, The eldest is a conference speaker and a praise dancer, and she worked in the school system for over 30 years. She is also married to a wonderful man. My little sister, the one I call Miss Intelligent, is also a conference speaker and teacher of women. She has been in the school system, teaching at-risks teens and junior-high-school students. She is blessed to have a husband who loves the Lord. They share in teaching the word of God, and he will soon become a licensed minister.

My baby brother is a minister of the gospel and a coach of a girls' softball team, and he has taken time to feed the homeless and preach the gospel in prisons. Our children are saved and grandchildren are covered by the blood of Jesus. I thank Him and praise Him for all that He has done.

Where would we be if we had not grabbed ahold of God's word? Where would we be if we had allowed the enemy of depression to destroy our minds, steal our joy, and take our peace? God's word helped us through this battle. It was by the grace of God. Let me encourage you, as this battle can be won through prayer, the word of God, medication, counseling, and/or therapy. I say the most important part is the word of God, because God's word will keep you, sustain you, and restore you when all your treatment is completed.

Writing "*The Enemy Depression*" has shown me how the real enemy of this world can take the form of an illness like depression to keep one bound. His purpose is to kill, steal, and destroy God's creation—us, His people. But because of God and who He is, I have seen the purpose He had for my life and my family as a whole. We are living that abundant life that the Lord promised. He said, "I will never leave you nor forsake you," yet we left him. I left him spiritually, physically, and mentally, but God stayed with us. Through all of life's challenges, the Lord delivered us.

"And we know that all things work together for the good of those who love God and are called according to his purpose." Romans 8:28

We are called by God, and He is not going to let us fall into the hands of the enemy. He will not let you, your family, or your loved ones fall prey to the enemy of depression. Get the word of God and hold fast to it.

AN INVITATION

I must acknowledge that not everyone shares the same faith or experiences as I do, especially in their relationship with the Lord Jesus Christ, the God of the universe. However, if you've encountered struggles similar to mine or are open to accepting Him into your life, I'd like to extend a simple invitation.

It goes as follows:

"Father, I acknowledge that I've fallen short of the glory you intended for me. I repent of any and all sins I've committed. Please come into my heart, be my Lord and Savior. Amen."

By choosing to say this prayer, you are welcomed into the Body of Christ. With this newfound faith, you can confront the battle of depression more effectively, knowing that you have God and all of heaven supporting you. Trust in the scriptures and the Word of God to guide you through this journey.

SCRIPTURE REFERENCE GUIDE

The following scriptures are promises of God to mend our broken hearts and help us through times of depression. They will offer restoration and a relationship with the Lord. He is our Creator, our Redeemer, and our Defender. When Jesus, himself, was led into the wilderness, He used the Word of God against the enemy. By His Word, the enemy has to flee.

John 4:13 – Whosoever drinks the water that I give will never thirst again
Matt 21:22 – Whatever you ask in prayer and belief
Psalm 51 – Have mercy on me O' Lord
Psalm 23 – The lord is my shepherd and I shall not want...
Luke 11:9-13 – Seek and you shall find, knock and the door will be opened
James 1:17 – Every good and perfect gift comes above
John 14:15 – And whatever you shall ask in my name I will do
Psalm 51:17 – The sacrifices of God are a broken spirit
Philippians 4:13 – I can do all things through Christ who gives me strength

SCRIPTURAL AFFIRMATIONS:

I am forgiven of all my sins and washed in the blood of the lamb – Ephesians 1:7
I am born of God and the evil one does not touch me – I John 5:18
I am a new creation in Christ – II Corinthians 5:17
I am the righteousness of God in Christ Jesus – II Corinthians 5:21
I am complete in Him who is the head of all principalities and powers – Colossians 2:10
I am more than a conqueror through him who loves me – Romans 8:37
I have the peace of God which Passes all understanding – Philippians 4:7
I am strengthened with all might according to his glorious power – Colossians 1:11

I am healed by the stripes of Jesus - Isaiah 53:6 – I Peter 2:24

No weapon formed against me can prosper — Isaiah 54:17

The Lord hides me in His pavilion and in the safety of His arms. — Psalm 27:5

I have been delivered from the power of darkness and translated into the kingdom of God's son; in whom I have redemption through His Blood, even the forgiveness of sins – Colossians 1:13-14

ACKNOWLEDGMENTS

First, to my Lord and savior Jesus Christ. Father, You know I really tried to be obedient, to listen, and to hear Your voice. Thank You for being patient with me.

To my husband, who prayed for me and confirmed that God wanted this book written to help those battling depression.

Then to my daughter who encouraged me each day as I struggled with my thoughts. To our granddaughter Jazzy, who attempted to read my book in rare form, giving me pointers to break it down so that it would be so much easier to read. I praise God for my friends who prayed and pushed me to get it done. Miss Nina, who offered to help me—I couldn't, as much as you wanted to! I had to pray for your healing instead. God bless you and heal you in the name of Jesus!

There are so many that I dare not mention names so as to not leave anyone out. To all of you who knew I was attempting this book, God bless and thank you for your prayers!

Last, to a man who is an author, preacher, and teacher of God's word, and a man who does not know me but came to a church I was attending two years ago. He said, "Someone is writing a book," and handed me his copy of "Don't Just Speak It, Write It" by Don Newman.

ABOUT THE AUTHOR

Dr. Sharon Harris is a wife, mother, grandmother, and GG. She is a bible teacher and minister of the Gospel of Jesus Christ.

Dr. Sharon retired from Gardner Community Health Center as a Registered Dental Supervisor and a Dental Assistant Instructor in California. Dr. Sharon received her degrees from San Jose City College, San Jose Christian College, and Sacramento Bible College and Seminary. She now serves at the Solaris Nursing Care

Facility in Florida and leads Saturday morning worship service and Tuesday devotionals.

Dr. Sharon enjoys serving people and leading others to Christ. In her ministry, *Rose of Sharon,* she shares her gifts of prayer, praise dance, and improv drama. When not serving you will find her at the ocean or near a lake watching the sun rise.

BIBLIOGRAPHY REFERENCE

Helping Hurting People, **Dr. Pauline Reeder**, *Director of Christian Education, Progressive Baptist Convention for New York State.*

The Bible, New King James Version, by God

The Bible Commentary

Henderson Ph. D, Jenny, & Shirley LCSW, Nadine, Feeling down?

London School of Economics, The Depression Report, the Center for Economics

Performance's Mental Health Policy Group, June 2006.

National Inst. Of Mental Health, June 2005

The Sam's Center for Optimal Performance, Depression / Anxiety, Jan. 2008

Time Magazine Special Report, A User's Guide to the Brain, Jan. 2007

USA Today

Segment.com

http://en.dictionary.org/wiki/despair

http:/www.depression.com

http://www.healthy.yahoo.com/depression-in children-and-teens

Bible Quiz, christians.net, 2004

Made in the USA
Las Vegas, NV
16 April 2024

88732186R00036